Foreword
By Abraham Lincoln

The pens and pencils normally found in school classrooms will work with the most common notebook papers to learn the basic letter shapes found in the back of this workbook. Students are encouraged to use the writing tools in their possession.

You can use calligraphy pens, such as the Panache®, goose or turkey quills and dip pens like the Speedball® "C" style dip pens on lessons in this workbook. There are many pages in this workbook about italic calligraphy and were made for calligraphers and for those wanting to improve their handwriting.

The book has letter style lessons. The models are examples of ideal forms and are something to aspire to. Models and styles are shown as examples. They are portraits of your future penmanship.

Stroke directions and numbers of strokes for each letter are provided before each lesson page.

Enjoy learning how to write by keeping a journal. You can look back and see your progress. Save the design ideas for a time when you are confident with the styles and shapes and have learned something about design and color.

Abraham Wesley Lincoln
Brookville, Ohio 45309-1207

Abraham Lincoln's
AN ITALIC CALLIGRAPHY WORKBOOK

An Introduction to
Handwriting and Calligraphy

ISBN 094203212-8

ISBN 0-942032-12-8

About the Book
An Introduction to Handwriting and Calligraphy

This is an introduction to learning the 14th Century italic handwriting styles we know as Italic Calligraphy. It is also an introduction to ordinary handwriting improvement.

People like Italy's Arrighi (1522) and Spain's Francisco Lucas (1577) were respected scribes and their work is responsible for all writing styles in use in English speaking countries today. Their styles can be done in a formal writing style or they can be used in everyday handwriting.

Lessons can be used as a guide or can be traced over.

Each letter of the alphabet is covered by itself, used in words and both letter and word space are included. The number of strokes required to make a letter are shown with pen nibs that indicate the number of individual strokes. The actual stroke direction is shown with lines and arrows.

There are chapters about design, layout and other styles, including italic for ball pens and pencil (These can also be used by tracing over the letters with a calligraphy pen).

You might consider taking the Skills – Achievement Survey as it is a reminder of those things important to scribes and calligraphers. See page 54.

You are encouraged to experiment with different calligraphy styles and use them in different layouts and designs to show your newly acquired writing skills.

Introduction
Things You Need to Know

How to determine guideline size

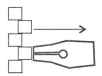

turn pen on side and make 5 marks to determine
how far apart each guideline is for that pen size

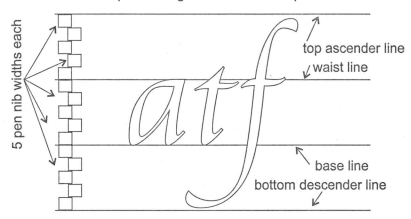

5 pen nib widths each

top ascender line

waist line

base line

bottom descender line

4

Paper placement

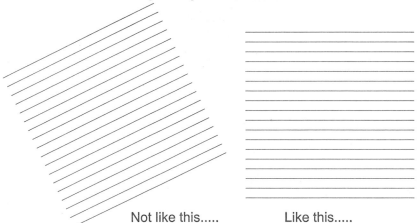

Not like this.....   Like this.....

Introduction
Things You Need to Know

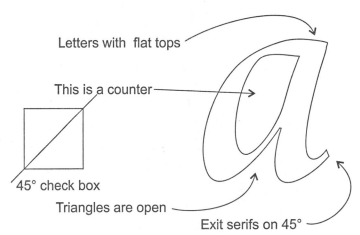

Letters with flat tops

This is a counter

45° check box

Triangles are open

Exit serifs on 45°

Models

Each lesson page has a model letter for the lesson. The model letters will show how that letter looks with related letters. The models are italic calligraphy styles.

Guidelines

Guidelines are used merely to keep your writing on a straight line across the page. The guidelines consist of a writing line. The line you write on is called the base line and the bottom of the letter rests on it. The other important line is the one right above the base line and one I call the waist line. It is to the tops of some letters the same as the base line is to all letters. Waist lines are used to keep the tops of lines of writing even and easier to read and that is the purpose of the base lines.

slant or slope line guide*

45° degree pen nib angle

Ascender Line
Waist Line
Base Line
Descender Line

If you picked out 4 lines on a sheet of notebook paper they are commonly all used in handwriting and have different names.

The topmost line or first line is the ascender line. All ascending letters stop here or are limited to this line height. The next line is the waist line and the one after that is the base line. Finally, the last line is the descender line. All letters with descenders use this line as a guide that shows where the descending letter stops.

Introduction
Things You Need to Know

Stroke Directions
The stroke direction matters only if you are
using a calligraphy pen and then only if you
happen to push the pen when it should be
pulled.

This is called "stroke direction" and is important
when making letters using a square cut pen or
quill.

Going the right way prevents the nib from
digging into the paper fibers and splattering ink.

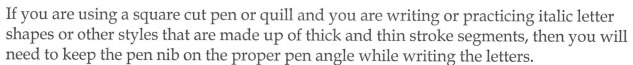

If you are using a square cut pen or quill and you are writing or practicing italic letter
shapes or other styles that are made up of thick and thin stroke segments, then you will
need to keep the pen nib on the proper pen angle while writing the letters.

The pen makes thick parts and thin parts as it goes
around the letter shape. It is automatic in most
instances but there are some styles that actually
requires the pen nib to be twisted or turned while the
letter stroke is being made.

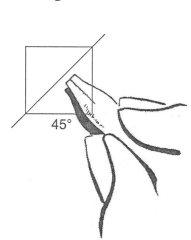

45°

Introduction
Things You Need to Know

Pen Angles

Pen angles matter when you use square cut pen nibs designed for lettering and calligraphy and you are trying to write a specific letter style.

Each style has a different pen-angle that should be used if you are trying to make what you are writing look like that particular style.

For <u>italic calligraphy</u> done with calligraphy pens, the pen should be placed on the paper on a 45° degree angle. A diagonal line through a square box can be used as a guide as a reminder of this rule.

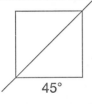

45°

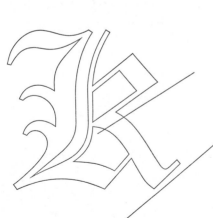

45° pen angles for italic

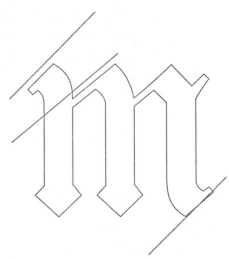

Fraktur uses other pen angles

Cloister uses other pen angles

Introduction
Things You Need to Know

Historical Models

Our handwriting alphabet is based on Roman historical models. Those forms are the basis of all modern handwriting styles. An early 1500s style is below.

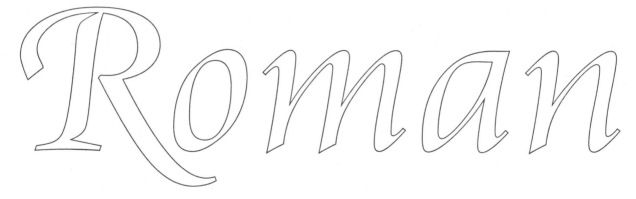

The alphabet itself remains the same but what you see today is the result of scribbling and changes people make in the Roman style. Modern roundhand styles use loops for cursive qualities and those may cause the appearance to seem different but the letters have the same basic shape. An early 1900s style is below.

Introduction
Things You Need to Know

Stroke Directions and More
Generally speaking, the same stroke directions are used with italic calligraphy pens, large sponge brushes or ball point pens.

The following pages show the directions as lines with arrows on one or both ends. If an arrow is on both ends that means it can be pushed left or right with the same result. The pages also show a pen point. If you see two pen points that means the letter is best made in 2 strokes of the pen. Three pens would indicate 3 strokes of the pen.

Most formal letters begin on the waist line except those with tall ascenders that begin on the topmost guideline.

I recommend you use Speedball® "C" style dip pens or fountain pen sets like the Panache® Basic and Master Calligraphy pen sets. Use the dip pens for all watercolor gouache paint that you use for calligraphy as the gouache would ruin the fountain pens.

You can use those inexpensive sponge brushes sold for painting trim in homes. They are chisel edged and can be used with paint, ink, watercolor, and anything else that leaves a mark. They will produce idea shapes just like your better fountain pens but on a much larger scale.

Lesson Material
Things You Need to Know

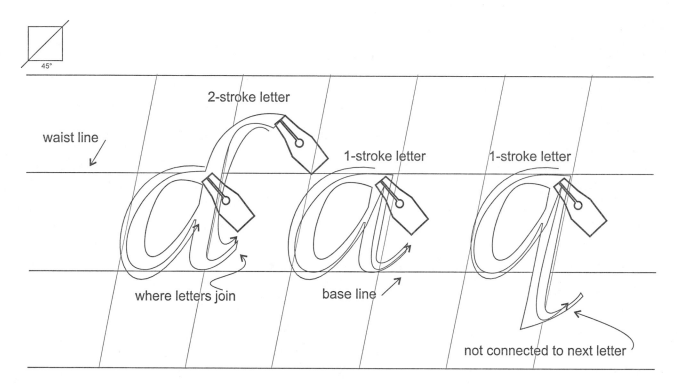

These letters begin on the waist line with the pen angle at 45 degrees. They have flat tops and all have open triangle areas. The counters are identical in each of these letters. They all slant or lean over to the right and they are not round but compressed and elliptical. Notice the "d" is made in 2 individual pen strokes in this formal style and the others are made in one pen stroke. Similar shaped letters have the same starting points.

Chapter 1 – Lesson 1
An Introduction to Handwriting and Calligraphy

Write the letters shown. Slow down. Use a small calligraphy pen when making the letters. The letters can be traced or written next to. Practice on notebook paper.

slant or slope line guide*

45°

abcdefghijklmnopqrstuvwxyƏz

adgq

daq

dag

aaa

dddd

qqqqq

*letters should not lean over more than this

Lesson 2
An Introduction to Handwriting and Calligraphy

The direction lines are those with arrow heads. The pen points show pen angle or start and finish points and the number of strokes to make the letter. One point is 1 stroke,

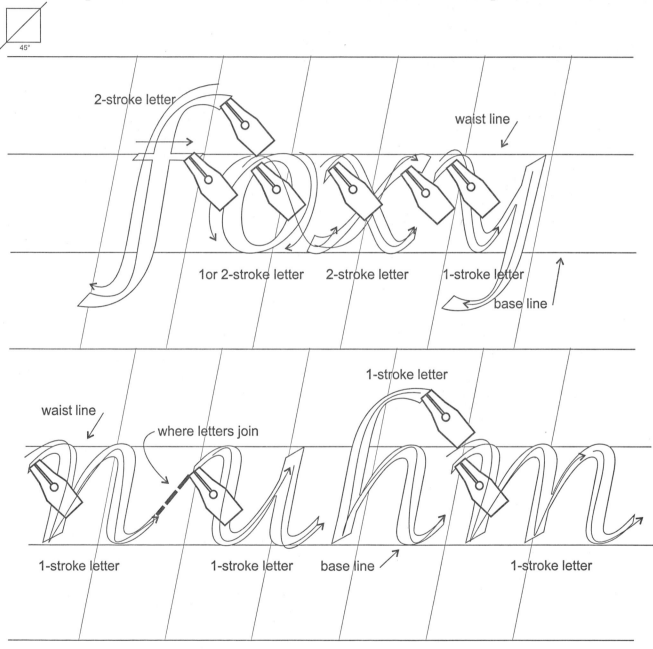

Lesson 3
An Introduction to Handwriting and Calligraphy

Slow down. Study the shape. Use a small calligraphy pen when making the letters. The letters can be traced or written next to. Practice on notebook paper.

nuhm

foxy

yxof

mhnu

nnn

mmm

fffxxx

Lesson 4
An Introduction to Handwriting and Calligraphy

The direction lines are those with arrow heads. The pen points show pen angle or start and finish points and the number of strokes to make the letter.

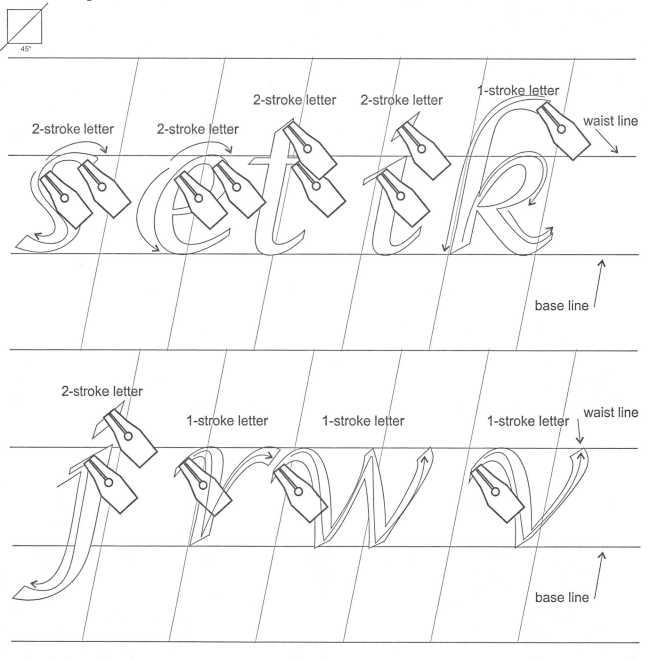

Lesson 5
An Introduction to Handwriting and Calligraphy

Watch things like space between letters and words. Notice the space between words is about equal to an "n" letter and between letters it is about equal to an "i" letter.

foxy

kites

sets to

kits

jar me

waved

mushed

Lesson 6
An Introduction to Handwriting and Calligraphy

The direction lines have arrow heads. The pen points show pen angle or start and finish points and the number of strokes to make the letter. One point is 1 stroke, etc..

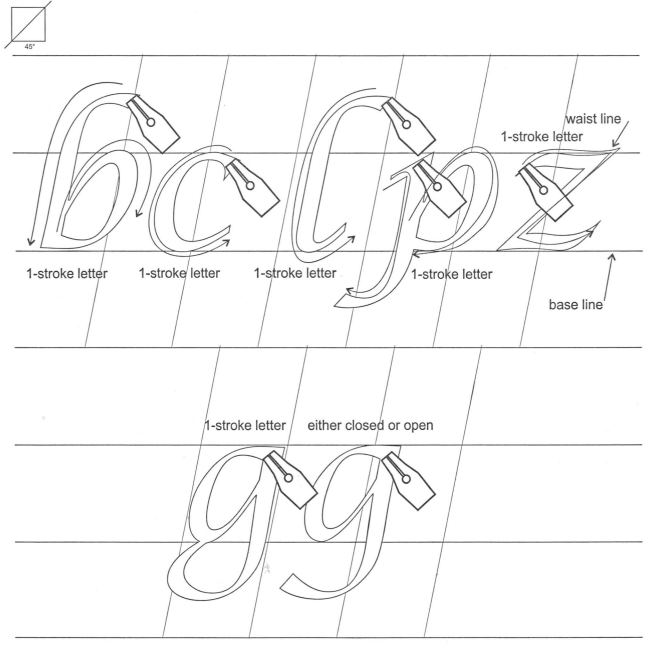

Lesson 7
An Introduction to Handwriting and Calligraphy

Watch things like space between letters and words. Notice the space between words is about equal to an "n" letter and between letters it is about equal to an "i" letter.

bclpz

natural

all of it

pale ghost

bitters

zombie

pet the dog

Lesson 8
An Introduction to Handwriting and Calligraphy

Those "hooked" ascender is where a cursive loop would hook on. Think about loops on ordinary handwriting and how a loop would attach.

armed

bakers

chocolate

dwaddle

peak

kindness

frank

Lesson 9
An Introduction to Handwriting and Calligraphy

Write these simple words using the letters already learned. Notice the amount of space between each word is about equal to an o or an n. I think "n" works best.

45°

nowadays

wish for it

drive up

wild thing

entire cup

total of 3

fright in me

Lesson 10
An Introduction to Handwriting and Calligraphy

If you are using a square cut quill or a small calligraphy pen then you should use the 45 degree check box to align your pen with before making letters.

it is time to go

let it go with it

me and you

we can do it

the ball game

hello to you

write away

Lesson 11
An Introduction to Handwriting and Calligraphy

Capitals are simple shapes but require more than a single stroke to finish. Refer to the models for the number of strokes and their direction.

Dear Jim,

Thank you,

Happy Days

Mr. and Mrs.

Dr. Gilbert

Sendai-shi

Japanese

Lesson 12
An Introduction to Handwriting and Calligraphy

ABCDEFGHIJKLMNOPQRSTUVWXYZ

Some pen manipulation is required to get finishes shown on flourishes

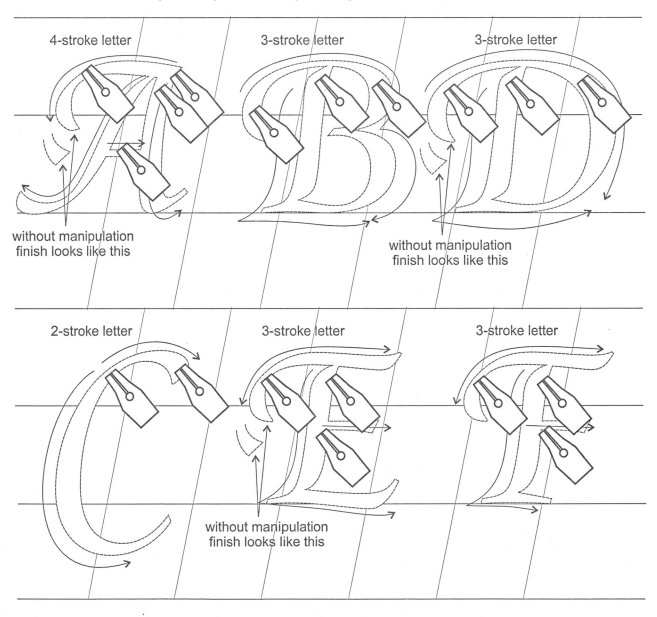

4-stroke letter

3-stroke letter

3-stroke letter

without manipulation
finish looks like this

without manipulation
finish looks like this

2-stroke letter

3-stroke letter

3-stroke letter

without manipulation
finish looks like this

Lesson 13
An Introduction to Handwriting and Calligraphy

Capitals are simple shapes but require more than a single stroke to finish. Refer to the models for the number of strokes and their direction.

45°

is it am Don.

she is Barb.

Fare twins.

Canary

February

Arched

Elf

Lesson 14
An Introduction to Handwriting and Calligraphy

Some pen manipulation is required to get finishes shown on flourishes

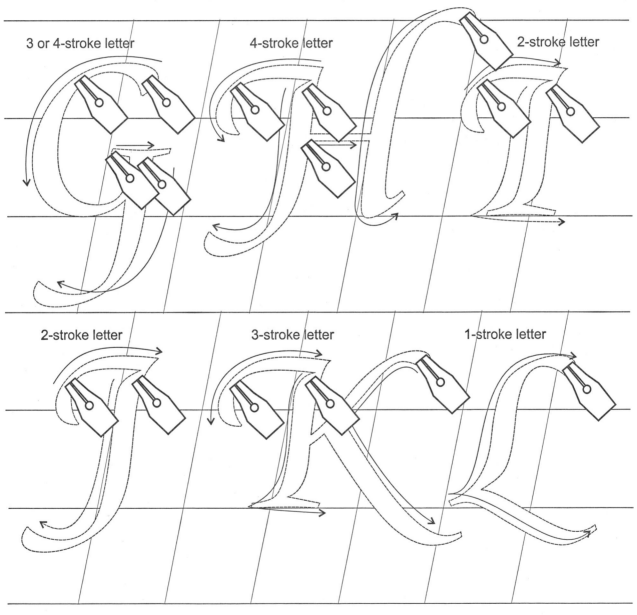

3 or 4-stroke letter   4-stroke letter   2-stroke letter

2-stroke letter   3-stroke letter   1-stroke letter

Lesson 15
An Introduction to Handwriting and Calligraphy

Refer to the models for the number of strokes and their direction.

Giddy

Hope

Island

Jupiter

Kingdom

Lavish

Ben Hur

Lesson 16
An Introduction to Handwriting and Calligraphy

Some pen manipulation is required to get finishes shown on flourishes

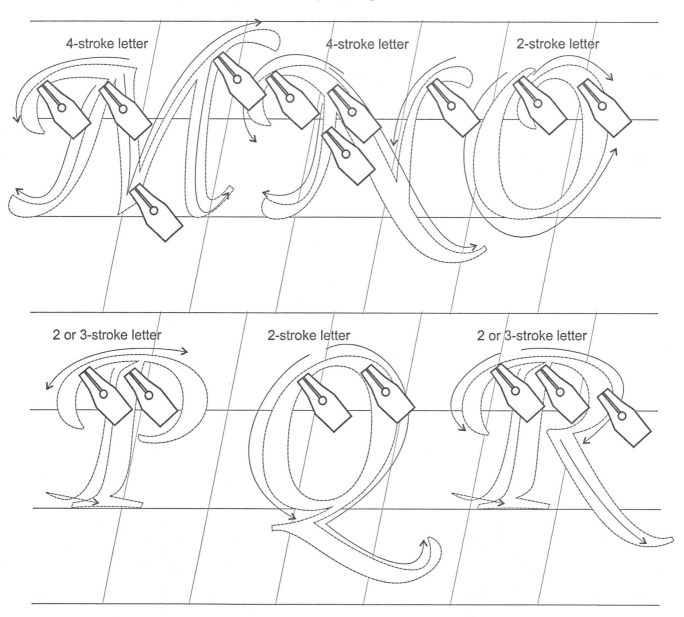

4-stroke letter   4-stroke letter   2-stroke letter

2 or 3-stroke letter   2-stroke letter   2 or 3-stroke letter

Lesson 17
An Introduction to Handwriting and Calligraphy

Swash capitals have no limit on how they might look but please keep all extensions natural and within reason. They are natural pen flourished parts and not drawn-out.

45°

Mr. & Mrs.

Dodge Neon

Oh Pat

Queen

Rancid

Dr. Tom

Nogales

Lesson 18
An Introduction to Handwriting and Calligraphy

Some pen manipulation is required to get finishes shown on flourishes

Lesson 19
An Introduction to Handwriting and Calligraphy

This is a modern italic calligraphy style that seems easier for beginners to write because the small letters do not have the traditional clubbed ascenders.

45°

Sam's

Tiny Yip

Uno Dos

Very Zoo-like

Waterfalls

Xacto knife

Omar

Lesson 20
An Introduction to Handwriting and Calligraphy

This italic style is quicker to write. It is a model similar to the 1577 Lucas style and is a kind of up and down saw-tooth movement. Use a small calligraphy pen nib The pen angle is less than 45 degrees.

5 pen nib widths

abcdefghijkl

mnopqrst

uvwxyz

abcdefghijklmnopqrstuvwxyz

Lesson 21
An Introduction to Handwriting and Calligraphy

This style is deliberate and while it retains the traditional shape it seems to lean more and appears quicker to write. The pen angle is slightly different making the down strokes thicker. Some pen manipulation may be required.

AAAA

Notice how the pen angle changes for different letter parts

BBBB

This is lettering and each letter is made of several separate parts.

CCCC

DDDD

EEEE

FFFF

GGGG

Lesson 22
An Introduction to Handwriting and Calligraphy

This is a modern italic calligraphy style that seems easier for beginners to write because the small letters do not have the traditional clubbed ascenders. If you don't like it you can skip this section.

HHHH

Notice how the pen angle changes for different letter parts

JJJJ

This is lettering and each letter is made of several separate parts.

gggg

KKKK

LLLL

MMMM

NNNN

Lesson 23
An Introduction to Handwriting and Calligraphy

This is a modern italic calligraphy style that seems easier for beginners to write because the small letters do not have the traditional clubbed ascenders. It is a loose style that appeals to some people.

oooo

Notice how the pen angle changes for different letter parts

pppp

This is lettering and each letter is made of several separate parts.

qqqq

RRRR

ssss

tttt

uuuu

Lesson 24
An Introduction to Handwriting and Calligraphy

This is a modern italic calligraphy style that seems easier for beginners to write because the small letters do not have the traditional clubbed ascenders.

vvvv

Notice how the pen angle changes for different letter parts

wwww

This is lettering and each letter is made of several separate parts.

xxxx

yyyy

tttt

zzzz

1234567890

Lesson 25
An Introduction to Handwriting and Calligraphy

When the style is seen in sentences it appears to be a modern calligraphy style with the same italic shapes. It has a texture about it that traditional italic calligraphy lacks.

above

camel

doubtful

enabled

framed

grateful

humble

Lesson 26
An Introduction to Handwriting and Calligraphy

Watch both letter and word spacing. Pay attention to triangle shapes and keep them open. See triangles in Notes section at back of book.

hinged

junkets

kingdom

landfill

milder

nameless

opals

Lesson 27
An Introduction to Handwriting and Calligraphy

This style looks almost the same when used to write words. The same rules apply for the beginner. Watch both letter and word spacing. Pay attention to triangle shapes and keep them open and remember your pen nib angle.

puckers

queensland

restaurant

sandwich

tumblers

uncles

velvet

Test
An Introduction to Handwriting and Calligraphy
1 minute duration

Below is a paragraph written in a loose version of a traditional italic style. It looks thinner because of the spacing and pen nib size. So choose a ball point or a small calligraphy style pen or quill and allow the ends of letters like "g" and "y" to curve up naturally in a flourish.

Remember pen angle, letter slant and spacing if you are using a square cut pen.

It is indeed a much more religious duty to acquire a habit of deliberate, legible and lovely penmanship in the daily use of the pen than it is to illuminate any quantity of texts.

	PRACTICE	FAIR	GOOD
☐ Pen Angle	_____	_____	_____
☐ Letter Slant	_____	_____	_____
☐ Letter Spacing	_____	_____	_____
☐ Appearance	_____	_____	_____
☐ Number of words completed in one minute			_____

Grade yourself. How did you do?

Chapter 2
An Introduction to Handwriting and Calligraphy

Styles are different. Styles are created by people who make letters different from model shapes. The following writing styles are all based on the same italic calligraphy forms but they all look so different.

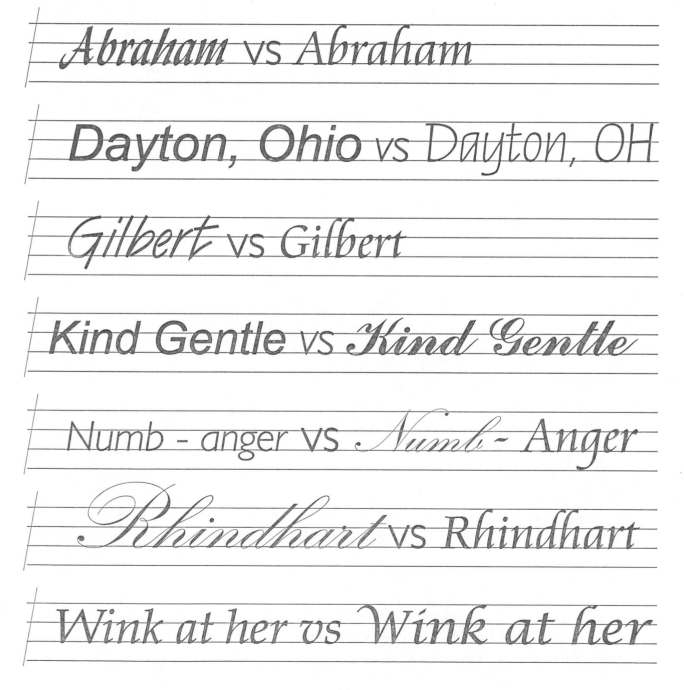

Chapter 2
An Introduction to Handwriting and Calligraphy

Styles are created by people who need to make their letters a little different from the model shapes. Here is a chance to compare styles and choose one you like.

Abcdefghijklmnopqrstuvwxyz

Abcdegfhijklmnopqrstuvwxyz

ABCDEFGHIJKLMNOPQ

RSTUVWXYZ 1234567890

ABCDEFGHIJKLMNOPQ

RSTUVWXYZ 1234567890

Experiment with styles

Chapter 2
An Introduction to Handwriting and Calligraphy

Styles often include stick-like strokes but the overall appearance remains an italic shape. Your style may be different but it will be your style and not mine. This is a drastic style but legible and easy to read and it is based on the same historical italic styles.

Abcdefghijklmnopqrstuvwxyz

A style is how you use models

1234567890

ABCDEFGHIJKLMNOPQRS

TUVWXY&Z

RSTUVWXYZ 1234567890

Experiment with styles

Chapter 3
About Quill Pens

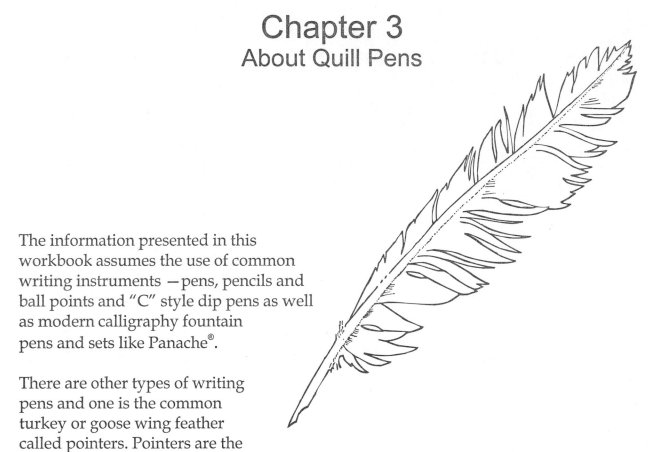

The information presented in this workbook assumes the use of common writing instruments — pens, pencils and ball points and "C" style dip pens as well as modern calligraphy fountain pens and sets like Panache®.

There are other types of writing pens and one is the common turkey or goose wing feather called pointers. Pointers are the largest three feathers on each wing. The right wing pointers curve back over the right-handed person's wrist and vice versa for the left-hand pointers. They must be dried out or cured before they are cut and prepared for writing.

All of the great documents were written with quill pens. Most were cut by the person doing the writing. When properly cut a goose quill pen is soft and flexible when used for writing. A turkey quill will be harder but produces equally elegant lines. I prefer turkey quills because I can lean on them a bit more and the resulting letters are not deformed by the added pressure.

Most quill pens were used with the feather part stripped off. What you see on desks in government offices are more for decoration. The real world used the barrel portion only.

Do not try to make pens for writing using tail feathers as they are too small. Use the wing feathers called "Pointers."

Chapter 3
About Cutting Quill Pens

This is basic information on how to cut a wing pointer and make a quill pen. It will take more than one try to make a pen that you can use.

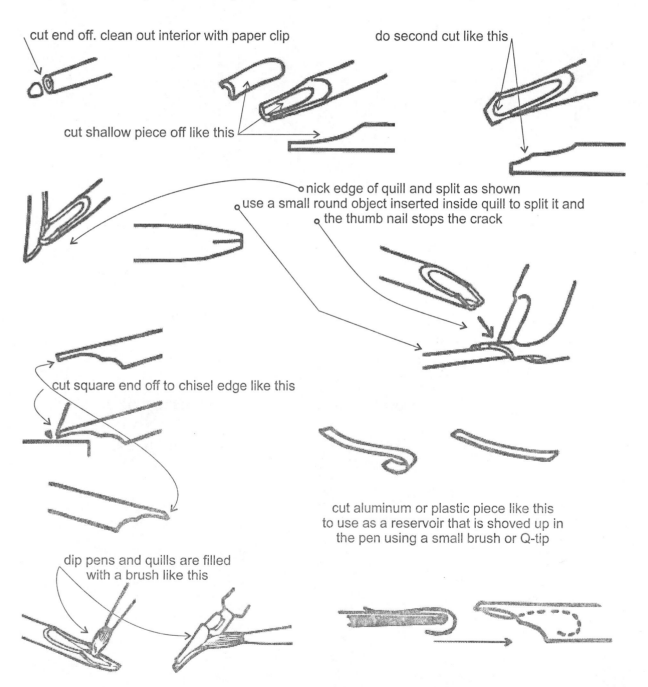

cut end off. clean out interior with paper clip

do second cut like this

cut shallow piece off like this

nick edge of quill and split as shown
use a small round object inserted inside quill to split it and
the thumb nail stops the crack

cut square end off to chisel edge like this

cut aluminum or plastic piece like this
to use as a reservoir that is shoved up in
the pen using a small brush or Q-tip

dip pens and quills are filled
with a brush like this

Chapter 3
About Pen Angle and Ink Flow

Writing was done on upright writing tables as shown in this illustration. The triangle represents the actual writing surface monks used.

The first drawing shows the quill is horizontal and the ink is level and will not make a blob when the quill touches the writing surface.

The second example shows the drop of ink at the point and it will make a blob when the quill touches the paper. This is how your quill will react when about to touch a flat writing surface. It will make a blob of ink instead of a nice letter shape. Use a sloped writing surface when using quills,

Scribal monks were able to control ink flow by tilting the pen up or down as shown by the second and third examples — when tilted down the ink backs away from the surface.

The last example represents a sloped writing desk. Notice the little finger and side of the palm will touch the desk when writing.

Chapter 3
About Calligraphy Layout

The principle of page layout is very old. Essentially, one draws a diagonal line from the left bottom corner to the top right corner of the page and along that diagonal line any square or rectangle shape will fit with its top right and bottom left corners touching the same diagonal line. If the area you want for text or art is too short it doesn't fit. If it is too long it doesn't fit. When it fits, that is the correct size text box for that page.

Any sheet of paper has a center. That is found by drawing diagonal lines from the four corners. Where they cross is the true center of that sheet of paper. Do not use the true center of the page as it creates an optical illusion of being too low. We offset that by dividing the page into tenths and the optical center is 4/10th of the way down from the top of the sheet.

optical center○

true center○

Medieval documents have special margins and those are not based on these centers.

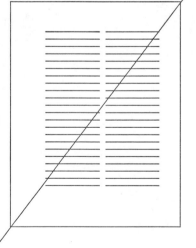

Old manuscripts are like this with two columns.

Chapter 3
About Calligraphy Layout

With pen and ink, brush and paint,
they form the form words from can't to ain't.

Dipping, flowing, swirling about—
letters and words forming with a Shout!

They seek to give, with graceful line,
the written word, true and fine.

So, I impart to you today:
Old calligraphers never die,
they just scribble away.

Written out by the author in 1977. Ray Hill quote. June 1977

Chapter 3
About Calligraphy Layout

𝕹ational 𝕾tudent 𝕱ilm 𝕱estibal

First Prize for Animation
Awarded to Robert Williams

Balance things on the right of center by things on the left sideor things on top by things that seem equal on the bottom. The mass on each side do not have to be equal. Layouts like this one are common.

Chapter 3
About Calligraphy Layout

Nancy Weinrich used her cartoon drawing skills to create characters like this one for books that the author wrote in the past. Notice the character appears balanced by the letters.

Chapter 3
About Calligraphy Layout

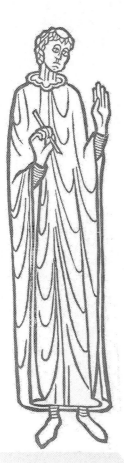

Dr. Otmar Premstaller, St. Georgen, Austria

Chapter 4
About Design

How you use what you have learned depends on what you intend to do. If you choose writing in a daily journal then do your best work beginning with italic calligraphy.

A journal and writing tools you can see and use should be easily seen as a reminder to write. I keep mine on my desk and use it daily. And I gave up trying to keep it perfect. I just grab a ball pen or a calligraphy fountain pen and jot down whatever and that's it. Sometimes the writing is careful and as neat as a pin and other times it is hurried and scatter-brained, but something is down on paper.

I use half size wire bound notebooks for journals and use a new one each year. I have many of them. They are a record of my life each day that I recorded things. I can look up things that happened in the past and sometimes that information was critical.

Prof. Dr. Albert Kapr, Leipzig, Germany

If you are going to make "arty" things that hang on walls or decorate notes then you will need to begin thinking about other larger writing tools and color. Dr. Kapr did many things in poster format like the example here.

Thinned-out watercolor and a large sponge house paint brush works for writing large letters. They work beautifully. They are also great to use in the classroom to write letters on blackboards using nothing more than water.

Experiment with cheap paper. I used to use classified newspaper for experiments and once I got a design that I liked then I began working on "real" paper with paints. You can determine what is best for you by trying different things.

Chapter 4
About Design

A business card size greeting

Designs used to decorate envelopes to people all over the world

Chapter 4
About Design

This design incorporates images of scribes from Egypt.
The combination makes a poster unusual. By the author.
Shown greatly reduced.

Chapter 4
About Design

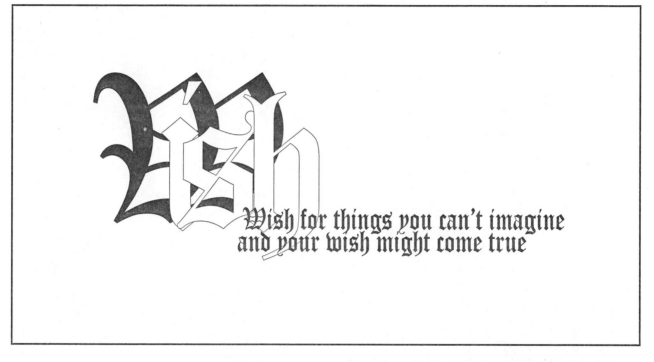

Experiment with styles and placement and sizes.

Skills — Achievements
An Introduction to Handwriting and Calligraphy

5 points for each yes score

Name _____ Date _____

Basic Concepts — Self Discipline	Yes	No
Correct posture	____	____
Pen angle	____	____
Paper position	____	____
Correct letter slant	____	____
Counters and triangles are open	____	____
Letter spacing correct	____	____
Word spacing correct	____	____
Writes all small letters from memory	____	____
Able to write all capital letters from memory	____	____
Can write a sentence using cursive or connected italic scripts	____	____
Has the ability to write a formal italic style with hooked ascenders and descenders	____	____
Can critique own work or the work of others properly	____	____

Cursive Writing — Fundamentals

	Yes	No
Can write 60 letters per minutes	____	____
Cursive slant does not exceed 15 degrees	____	____
Cursive letter joins are on 45 degrees or connecting line is thinnest	____	____
In cursive writing the space between letters is than in formal writing	____	____
Maintains legible forms while writing at speed	____	____

Creative Writing Habits

	Yes	No
Knows the vocabulary of calligraphy and uses it	____	____
Writes lines out in pencil on separate paper and checks spelling and word meanings	____	____
Uses a dictionary to look words up and doesn't make mistakes	____	____
Demonstrated knowledge of page layout and design	____	____
Has used colors in handwriting in ink or watercolors	____	____
Experiments with designs and color and lettering sizes	____	____

Basic Knowledge Applied

	Yes	No
7 to 10 degree letter slant throughout any exercise	____	____
If square cut nib is used to write italic is the pen nib able on 45 degrees through letters	____	____
Are counters alike or similar	____	____
Are triangles alike or similar and open	____	____
Do flourishes look natural and not drawn out	____	____
Totals	____	____

check yourself out

Chapter 5 – Lesson 1
An Introduction to Handwriting and Calligraphy

Simple line italic alphabets are ideal for ball pen and pencil users. Italic calligraphy pen users can trace-over the letters. The letters have the same shape as 14th Century Italic but are minus all decoration or serifs. The slant lines can be used as a guide for letter slant and letter widths.

abcdefghijklmnopqrstuvwxy&z

slant or slope line guide

adgpbcq

note similarity of letter shapes

nhn

hnbpr

test kit

quarter

vwxyz

Lesson 2
An Introduction to Handwriting and Calligraphy

Simple line italic alphabets are ideal for ball pen and pencil users but can be traced over by using a calligraphy pen. The letters have the same shape as 14th Century Italic but are minus all decoration or serifs. The slant lines can be used as a guide for letter slant

abcdefghijklmnopqrstuvwxyz

slant or slope line guide

opqrst

xyzamd

soaps

wisdom

gardens

diamonds

Lesson 3
An Introduction to Handwriting and Calligraphy

Slow down. Pay attention to the slant of letters and the space between them.

slant or slope line guide

ABCDEFGHIJKLMNOPQRST

UVWXYZ & 1234567890

1950 — 1998 — 2000 — 2004

Lesson 4
An Introduction to Handwriting and Calligraphy

Slow down. Use a pencil or ball point when making these letters. You may use a small calligraphy pen and trace over these skeletal shapes.

slant or slope line guide

Absent

Bishop

Chelse

Dover

Events

Fishers

Garter

Lesson 5
An Introduction to Handwriting and Calligraphy

Slow down. Use a pencil or ball point when making these letters. You may use a small calligraphy pen and trace over these skeletal shapes.

Heaven

Islands

Jumper

Kissing

Lincoln

Musher

Nasty

Lesson 6
An Introduction to Handwriting and Calligraphy

Slow down. Use a pencil or ball point when making these letters. You may use a small calligraphy pen and trace over these skeletal shapes.

Opinion

Pucker

Queens

Rushes

Strobes

Trucker

Uncles

Lesson 7
An Introduction to Handwriting and Calligraphy

Slow down. Use a pencil or ball point when making these letters. You may use a small calligraphy pen and trace over these skeletal shapes.

Vehicle

Wrecks

Xactos

Yellows

Zebras

1987 street

2654

Lesson 8
An Introduction to Handwriting and Calligraphy

You may use a small calligraphy pen and trace over these skeletal shapes or use a ball pen and copy the shapes.

3201

abcdef

ghijkl,

mnopq.

rstuvw:

xyz?!'

"&"123's

Lesson 9
An Introduction to Handwriting and Calligraphy

Do your best to use the lines to write the letters shown. Slow down. Use a pencil or ball point when making these letters. You may use a small calligraphy pen and trace over these skeletal shapes.

ABCD

EFGHI

JKLMN

OPQRS

TUVWX

Y&Z

( ) $ %

Lesson 10
An Introduction to Handwriting and Calligraphy

Do your best to use the lines to write the letters shown. Slow down. Use a pencil or ball point when making these letters. You may use a small calligraphy pen and trace over these skeletal shapes. Watch space between words and letters.

carving the

running to

walk over

summer

dolls are

prep school

it is a tie

Useful Information
An Introduction to Handwriting and Calligraphy

Big letters should look like small ones and to make them with the same proportions, you will need to scale them up using the width of the pen nib as a guide. The distance, for example, in between guidelines (waist and base) is about 5 pen nib widths. There are 5 for the ascender and 5 for the descender area whether you use this space or not — allow it. So 1 line of writing requires 15 pen nib widths. You may have to use sponge paint brushes to duplicate the shapes for large lettering but the height is still figured the same.

See page 4.

Letters with similar shapes — *abcdgpq*

Letters branch out the same — *ihnmrluy*

Letters with diagonal lines — *VWXZ*

Letters with bowls — *oek*

Letters with crossed parts — *ft*

Letters with all curves — *OS*

Letters with diagonal lines — AKMNVWXYZ

Letters with bowls and straight lines — BDGPRU

Letters with diagonal lines — VWXZ

Round shapes — CQOS

Straight lines — EFHIKLMNTVWXYZ

Useful Information
An Introduction to Handwriting and Calligraphy

Drying feathers.
Hand in bundles in the attic. You can also do it the old fashioned way by covering them with sand and heating the sand. Be sure to scrape off the outer membrane or the pen will never work properly and it will be harder to split the nib. Also be sure to take out the inner pith. Use a small hook for this purpose.

Branching vs arching.
An arch is made in two strokes. A branch is made in one stroke of the pen without lifting it off the paper.

Actually, the act of lifting the pen off the paper when you are making letters is considered "lettering" and is not handwriting or calligraphy.

Writing Motion.
When a person writes, the arm moves on the forearm muscle. This is the natural writing motion. This is a back and forth motion and try to imagine the teeth of a saw as the motion you are trying to mimic.

Finger or Wrist Motion.
Finger or wrist motion should be avoided.

The Best Motion.
It is best to combine forearm motion with some wrist motion. This is less tiring and is easier to control and that results in lines of writing that are nearly identical in their visual appearance.

Warm Up.
A warm up session should be done each day before writing. This is a forearm motion while doing groups of u's and n's. uuuuuuuuu nnnnnnnnnn

Lesson Plan
An Introduction to Handwriting and Calligraphy

Briefly describe what you are going to cover in a writing session and create a list of tools and supplies required to complete the lesson.

Time _____ Hours
Book _____
Paper _____
Pens _____
Inks _____
Colors_____

Work to be done

_____
_____
_____
_____
_____
_____
_____
_____
_____
_____
_____
_____
_____

Evaluation (Did the lesson work or how can it be improved)

_____
_____

Teacher _____ Date _____

Some flourished capitals
An Introduction to Handwriting and Calligraphy

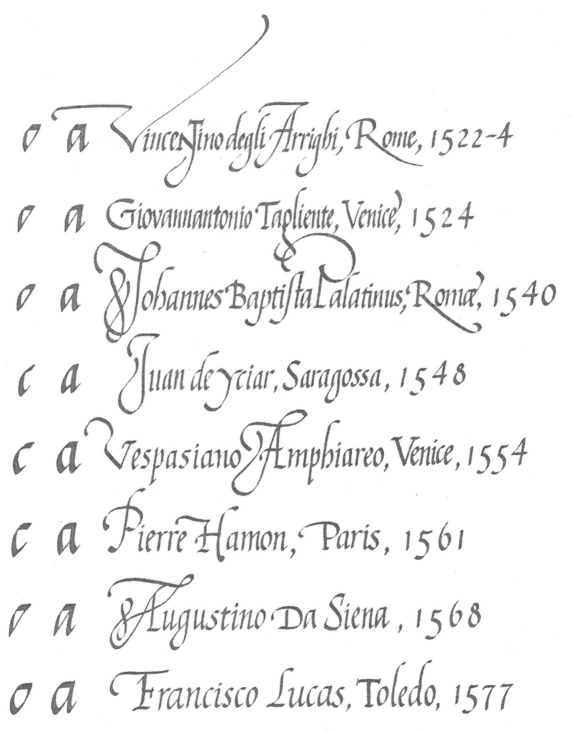

o a Vincenzino degli Arrighi, Rome, 1522-4

o a Giovannantonio Tagliente, Venice, 1524

o a Johannes Baptista Palatinus, Roma, 1540

c a Juan de yciar, Saragossa, 1548

c a Vespasiano Amphiareo, Venice, 1554

c a Pierre Hamon, Paris, 1561

o a Augustino Da Siena, 1568

o a Francisco Lucas, Toledo, 1577

Italic capitals by the author from various Renaissance scribes. Note the shape of the "a"

Some flourished capitals
An Introduction to Handwriting and Calligraphy

Dear Colleagues

I'm very glad to bring the hearty greetings from Finland,
the Country of the Northern Lights, Frost and the Midnight
Sun. My name is Hannu Paalasmaa and with the assistance
of my highly appreciated Colleague and Friend,
Mr. Villu Toots, Estonia, I've had a nice opportunity
to get acquainted with your Scribe Magazine. Like Estonia
You probably know, even Finland is a very small country
in northern Europe. Nevertheless in Finland we have
plenty of persons being interested in Calligraphy and
beautiful lettering. I'm working as the teacher of Calligraphy in Finland, but my main occupation is the head
of the book artists in Yleisradio, Tv 2 (Finnish television,
channel two).

I am in friendly relations with many famous
Enthusiasts of Calligraphy, and letters passed between
us regularly for years, concernig the professional
questions. Mr. Villu Toots from Tallinn is my Teacher
for years.

In Great Britain and West Germany, for example,
I have good Friends in Calligraphy, and now I should
like to be acquainted with american colleagues in lettering.
I know Mr. Paul Freeman is a superb craftsman, and
i guess you have thousands of specialists

in the U.S.

By Hannu Paalasma, Finland

Some flourished capitals
An Introduction to Handwriting and Calligraphy

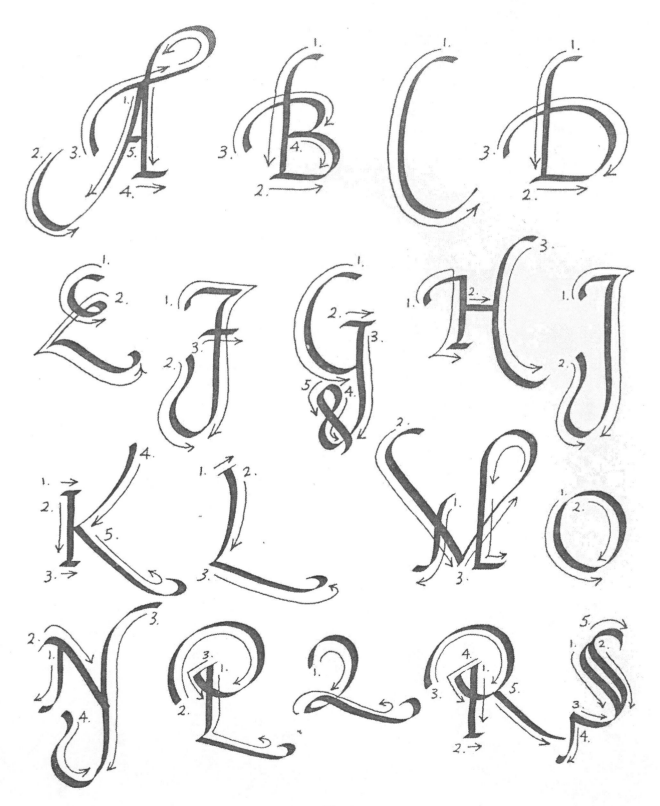

Some flourished capitals
An Introduction to Handwriting and Calligraphy

Some flourished capitals
An Introduction to Handwriting and Calligraphy

These majuscules are the ones used by most of the masters in their manuals.

No clearly defined rule related to numbers of strokes per letter, or their

ultimate size is given. They did suggest making them upright. Do not

make them lean over very much. You will not find very much deviation

between them. Use elaborate capitals at beginning paragraphs.